AT
THIS
POINT
IN
RHYME

TO MY COLLABORATORS
IN THE THEATRE

Fred (best of all possible words) Saidy
along with
Henry Myers and Sig Herzig
and to all my
(best of all possible notes)
composers
Harold Arlen, Vernon Duke, Burton Lane,
Jay Gorney, Jule Styne, Sammy Fain, Jerome Kern,
and my first
college partner in rhyme
Ira Gershwin

AT THIS POINT IN RHYME

E. Y. HARBURG'S POEMS

CROWN PUBLISHERS, INC. NEW YORK

Some of the poems in this collection were published in the *New York Herald Tribune,* *Saturday Review, The Churchman, Variety,* and *Hollywood Reporter.*

Inquiries should be addressed to Crown Publishers, Inc., One Park Avenue, New York, N.Y. 10016.

Published simultaneously in Canada by General Publishing Company Limited

Printed in the United States of America

Library of Congress Cataloging in Publication Data

Harburg, Edgar Y   1896-
        At this point in rhyme.

        CONTENTS: View from a flying saucer.—To be accompanied by cathedral organ.—Little drops of Watergate. [etc.]
        I. Title.
PS3558.A6A9   811'.5'4   76-22711
ISBN 0-517-52727-8

Book Design: Huguette Franco

THANK YOU, MARIE MARU

The title is vital
And so is Marie
The lady named Saidy
Who sparked it for me.

CONTENTS

TO EDELAINE

Her courage and compassion,
Her wisdom, warmth, and wit,
These are all the contents
In my survival kit.

THE FAR-OUT GENERATION

The freak-out,
The flop-out,
The psyche-out,
The drop-out.

The black-out,
The fall-out,
The conk-out,
The cop-out.

The wipe-out,
The sweat-out,
The strike-out,
The sell-out.

Are warning
The world we
Should all get
The hell out.

THE ODDS-ON FAVORITE

To make the longest story terse,
Be it blessing, be it curse,
The Lord designed the universe
    With built in obsolescence.
Each planet, comet, star, and sun
Enjoys a brief atomic run,
Erupting when its course is done,
    With cosmic incandescence.

Astronomers aver some day
Our solar star will blaze away,
There'll be a glorious display
    Of sunburst helium masses.
Our little planet earth below
Will be a pyrotechnic show
Of blazing hydrogen aglow
    With thermonuclear gases.

Thank God, this great combustion day
    Is many billion years away
So, as philosophers all say,
    Why fret . . . why fume . . . why worry?
A billion moons will wane and wax,
Sit down . . . make out your income tax . . .
Buy stocks, be calm . . . enjoy . . . relax
    For God is in no hurry.

But oh my friends, I have a hunch
That man may beat God to the punch.

HEAVENLY VAULTS

Where banks all look like temples,
  And temples look like banks,
Where does one count his blessings?
  Where does one offer thanks?

You sense the holy places
  By the faces in the ranks,
The bankrupt in the temples,
  The worshipful in banks.

MUSIC ON THE ROCKS

Hail the songs—the latest rages
  Dripping from guitar and pen,
All are destined for the ages—
  Like, I mean, from five to ten.

ECOLOGY IN A COUNTRY CHURCHYARD

The sulphured smog floats slowly o'er the lea,
    Across the sinking sun the soot is whirled.
The oil slick sparkles on a silvered sea,
    The serpent jet smoke skyward is unfurled.
My extra sinus perceptivity
    Tells me the world is not long for this world.

AND NEVER THE TWAIN SHALL MEET

Some are born in palaces,
Some are born in mangers,
Not all the Church's chalices
Nor all the Hebrew tallises,
Can heal the psychic calluses
That separate these strangers.

ALL THE NEWS THAT'S FIT TO PRINT

Blind man selling papers
    Seek, and you shall find
Pennies for your headlines—
    And thank the Lord you're blind.

SUREFIRE CANDIDATE

My candidate is heaven-sent,
　　He's hailed from east to west,
They drafted him for president
　　By popular request.

He's everybody's favorite son
　　From Sea to shining sea,
If there's a savior, he's the one
　　To raise our GNP.

He's loved by all the common folk,
　　He is the people's gem,
Their hope is in this sturdy oak,
　　His trust is all in them.

He greets the wildly cheering throng
　　On sidewalk, porch, and roof,
His voice is sure, his faith is strong,
　　His vest is bulletproof.

LETTER TO MY GURU

If this planet is a sample,
Or a preview if you will,
Or a model demonstration
Of the great designer's skill,
　　I say without hesitation,
　　"Thank you, no reincarnation."

STAR CROSSED

A little child somewhere on earth,
   Wishing on a star,
Wishes on Aquarius—
   His good luck reservoir.

Another on Aquarius,
   Wishes from afar
Upon a little star called Earth,
   Where all good wishes are.

THE FARE-THEE-WELL STATE

The people live on welfare,
The moguls live on oilfare,
The generals live on warfare,
Can anything be more fair?

THEY CAN'T BE ALL BAD

A world without the Reds
 Would be so doloroso.
No spies beneath our beds
 No headlines furioso.

No news, no hues, no cries
 To hypo the consumers.
No stocks to fall and rise
 Depending on peace rumors.

No fun for FBI
 No wherewithal for science,
No orders to supply
 Our big industrial giants.

No arms, no subs, no fleet,
 No anti-Commie comics,
No boom, no deals in wheat,
 In fact, no economics.

So orchids for Ivan!
 And roses for Natasha!
Let luxury roll on!
 Thank God for Godless Russia.

STRIKE THREE

A broken clock can tell the time
Correctly twice a day.
Astrologers, like broken clocks,
Are clairvoyant that way.

THE PAUSE THAT DEPRESSES

I scan the world at seventy-four
And after a double take,
I find that life is a state of war—
And peace is a coffee break.

ANAGRAM

"Tax exempt," "tariff," "parity,"
Are words you can scramble and switch,
However they fall, they spell "charity"
For the rich.

FROM YOUTH TO EUTHANASIA

Between the doctor and the priest
    Man does a double dive,
The priest wants youth to act as dead
    When nature wants him live.

And when the geriatric hulk
    Is wearied, sick, and bled,
The doctors strive to keep him live
    Though nature wants him dead.

OF THEE I SING—BABEL

Build thee more stately mansions, little man,
    More grandioso—more gargantuan.
But as the towers rise and derricks roar,
    Remember, there was once a dinosaur.

HIRSUTE OF HAPPINESS

The heads of state
Have doomed our fate,
The world is not in clover.
But are they really
Heads of state
Or merely necks haired over?

ON A CLEAR DAY
FROM MOUNT WILSON
YOU CAN SEE
WATTS

With magic gear through stratosphere
    Beyond the stars we grope,
But there's more to be found
    In the drop of a tear
Than there is in a telescope.

MY ART BELONGS TO DA DA

Today when art is money,
    And money colors art,
Oh, how shall we distinguish
    The goddess from the tart?

We thrive on fad and hoax and shock,
    But art outlives all cults.
Fad lives by the tick o' the clock
    Art, by the beat o' the pulse.

TAKE A LETTER TO JOYCE KILMER

You said you thought you'd never see
A poem lovely as a tree.

Yet here they stand for miles around
With gruesome branches, wired for sound,

Relaying trivialities
Where singing leaves once caught the breeze.

What greed so vile could play a joke
So low upon a mighty oak?

What mind could desecrate a birch
That stood more awesome than a church?

You said that there could never be
A poem lovely as a tree.

You never saw the trees I see
Transplanted by AT&T.

ALL RIOT ALONG THE POTOMAC

Poverty, war, pollution,
    Our Congress knows the score;
In fact, there's no solution
    They have no problem for.

A PUN TO PONDER ON

The whole human race
Could be living in grace
In a world that is lush and luxurious,
If the corporate boor,
Called the entrepreneur,
Were a little less entrepenurious.

PROSPECTS FOR A HAPPY NEW YEAR

Jovial Jan. and frivolous Feb.
Arrive with their sniffles and sneezes.
    March comes around
    With its vaporized sound
Of rhonchial, bronchial wheezes.

April's sweet showers are great for the flowers
But hell on the pelvis arthritic;
    And May, on the wing
    With her fevers of spring,
Lays you out on the couch analytic.

June and her roses play havoc with noses,
And ditto with larynx allergic;
    And jolly July
    With her poisonous I-
Vy defies all your curses non-clergic.

And now, amigitos, comes Aug. with mosquitos—
(Oh heaven knows where she has kept 'em)
    And Aug. turns to Sept.
    With her weeds still unswept
And Sept. goes to work on your septum.

Oct! is the sober sad cry for October
When psyches are fragile as tree leaves;
      They see through the soot
      That our fortunes, dear Brut-
Us, are not in the stars but the tea leaves.

Neurotic November creeps into December
With chilblains, depression, and flu . . .
      But the spirit says, "Blast
      It! It's Christmas at last,
And a happy New Year to you!"

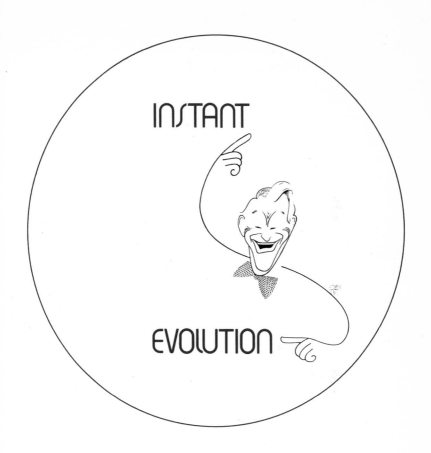

ADVANCED TECHNOLOGY AND SIDE EFFECTS

From Abacus to Computer,
Caveman to Neuter,
To final cataclysm?
Man—anachronism.

WE'VE COME A LONG WAY, BUDDY

An ape, who from the zoo broke free,
Was cornered in the library
With Darwin tucked beneath one arm,
The Bible 'neath the other.

"I can't make up my mind," said he,
"Just who on earth I seem to be—
Am I my brother's keeper
Or am I my keeper's brother?"

WE'VE COME A LONG WAY, BOOB...EE

Sexual revolution—during the 1930s, the official movie censor Mr. Breen
banned actresses from appearing on screen in sweaters. This was a puritan
reaction to the havoc caused by Lana Turner, the original sweater girl. This
poem was first printed in *Variety* in 1936.

When last he swung his busy ax
On movie aphrodisiacs
The conscientious censor Mr. Breen,

Decided that a stitch in time
Would save both poor and rich, in time,
    And thenceforth ruled all sweaters off the screen.

Somebody wrote a letter on . . .
"It's better with a sweater on . . ."
    And that gave Mr. B. no end of pain.
Which started this to-do of course;
Though everybody knew of course
    We're sisters under the (excuse it) skein.

And so it's . . . do your guzzlin' now
In linen, tweed, and muslin now,
    Emote your stuff in organdy or tulle.
He said—"In God we trust my lads,
But over any bust my lads
    We may not, no we dare not, pull the wool."

Oh you still can nip and tussle
With a muscle in a bustle,
    Or a bosom in a bale of duvetyn;
But you may not pull the gross up
With a knit-one, purl-one close up
    Of a wild and woolly weskit on the screen.

You can lap dissolve your thing-ums
In gay calicos or ginghams,
    Or accent your big broad "A"'s in velveteen;
And to meet the final hurdle
You can still let boy meet girdle—
    But boy cannot meet sweater on the screen.

TO DAVID—JUST BORN

When David slew Goliath,
When David wrote a psalm,
Whoever thought of him as once
    A plasmic blob in Mom?

But heaven in her wisdom,
And nature in her science
Can make a little molecule
    Rise up and slay the giants.

FROM WHENCE TO HENCE

Man is the coincidence
    Of accidents and consequence,
    A paradox of small events
        Forever fighting impotence.

With science and belligerence
    He battles for significance,
        His fortress and his one defense—
        The arrogance of ignorance.

TRANSCENDENTAL DEVIATION

Each day I wake with high resolve
    To grow mature and to evolve.
Each night upon my bed I fall
    And back into the womb I crawl.

WE IS MARCHIN'

Nature is a copiously
    Hopeful cornucopia
Of protoplasmic organisms
    Groping for utopia.

MICHAEL, ROW THE BOAT ASHORE!*

From womb to Tomb,
From birth to earth,
Man labors with ambition
To stretch his throb
Of life from ob-
Stetrician to mortician.

He'll snatch a score
Of days, or more,
From out the cosmic chasm,
Alas to squirm
From sperm to worm,
Then back to protoplasm.

From womb to tomb,
From sperm to worm,
The cocky and the proud
Drunk with science,
Flaunt defiance
From the diaper to the shroud.

From sperm to worm,
They reaffirm
That man is not time's slave;
But none has cast
A shadow past
The cradle to the grave.

34

*Negro spiritual

Man cures more ills
With magic pills
And miracles galore,
Yet round the cor-
Onary's door
There looms the coroner.

From dust to dust
In God they trust
Yet never grow the wiser,
That e'en the wise
Can only rise
From wise to fertilizer.

From seed to weed,
From weed to seed
They circle and recycle.
In jets they go,
But finally row
The boat across with Michael.

MIRACLE

We're wise to prestidigitators,
We're hip to all theatrics,

We know how rabbits turn to doves
In all the magic hat tricks,

But how did Mary's manger
Turn into the posh St. Patrick's?

FROM ETERNITY TO HERE

"Is there life after death?"
              Used to worry Aunt Emma.
"Is there life after birth?"
              Is her present dilemma.

BLUE CHIPS IN THE SKY

He made his millions milking slums,
              And kindred operations,
Then left his money to the Church-
              Of-All-Denominations,
He dealt in safe investments,
              Good returns with long endurance;
His heaven was a branch of
              The Hereafter Life Insurance.

HOW ODD OF GOD

How odd of God
To choose the Jews
Who'd choose a God
That chose to choose
Disciples who eschew
The Jews!

RODIN—PROPHET OR PRANKSTER?

A reader of palms in the Met Museum
Came upon Rodin's hand of God,
He studied each line—each crease—each seam,
And then remarked with a solemn nod:
"This life line that I seem to trace
Tells me God is a terminal case."

THE MAN WHO HAS EVERYTHING

For a halo up in heaven
    I have never been too keen.
Who needs another gadget
    That a fellow has to clean?

A TOEHOLD ON DIVINITY

Before me, the horizon rings the ocean,
Barefoot on the beach I stand astride
To greet the madcaps of perpetual motion
That scamper up the shore and leave the tide.

They leap up . . . kiss my toes . . .
    Then back they lope;
Can this be what it feels like
    To be Pope!

LAST RIGHTS

Exxon and Mobil Oil,
And one clear call for me!
And may there be no
    offshore drills
When I put out to sea.

A SAINT . . . HE AIN'T

Good St. Paul and Vincent Peale
Are men of wholly different steel,
  Yet both of holy calling.
St. Paul is most appealing
And Peale is most appalling.

SATAN TO THE RESCUE

This small bit of mud, revolving in space,
Would be an abysmal and dismal old place,
But thanks to the genius who first thought of sin,
This here is a dear little sphere to be in.

So hand him a halo,
Don't snub him a snub,
An Oscar, an Emmy
For old Beelzebub.
Yes, hand him a halo,
A halo, my lad,
But never bedevil the devil egad.

When husband is bored, and ditto the wife,
The demon's the cream in the coffee of life.
The best things on earth, are inevitably
Immoral,
Illegal,
And fattening,
And foolish,
Illicit,
And mis-
Understood—
But good!

Oh pity the parson, and pity his kin,
Should he fail to provide the transgressor.
How could they have saints if they didn't have sin?
Imagine their panic
Without this satanic
Professor.

The sermon is quaint—the moral is droll,
Both Plato and Pluto are good for the soul.
Let truth be untrammeled and sham be unshammed
And he who bedevils the Devil be damned.

HISTORY LESSON

This we learn from Watergate:
    That almost any creep'll
Be glad to help the government
    Overthrow the people.

NO EVIL IN THE OVAL ROOM

The White House has an oval room
Designed with cunning care,
    So any wily president
    Who happens to be resident
Could ne'er be cornered there.

THE TAPEWORM TURNS

    Spy not on thy brothers
    For power or pelf,
    He who bugs others
    Soon buggers himself.

IDENTITY CRISIS

Milhous Ben-Nixon in his royal tower
Awoke one night from a deep dream of power,
And saw within the moonlight of his room
A shadow with a peace-plaque glowing in the gloom.
He could not discern the form or face,
But he knew 'twas someone from outer space—
Some long-haired peacenik, some pinko poet,
The weird beard tells it and the peace words show it.
"You," cried Nixon, "may be someone from
Berkeley, Harvard, or kingdom come—
But to me you're nothin' but a campus bum!"
Just then Pat rubs her eyes and wheezes—
"My God, Dickie, you're talking to Jesus!"

BIOLOGY BITES THE DUST

Genetics is a puzzling science,
It doesn't merit much reliance.
Pygmies have been spawned by giants.

From geniuses of all degrees,
Come many mediocrities—
Consider Spiro Agnew, please,
Whose lineage is Socrates.

THE ENEMY LIST

Lives of great men all remind us
        Greatness takes no easy way,
All the heroes of tomorrow
        Are the heretics of today.

Socrates and Galileo,
        John Brown, Thoreau, Christ, and Debs
Heard the night cry "Down with traitors!"
        And the dawn shout "Up the rebs!"

Nothing ever seems to bust them—
        Gallows, crosses, prison bars;
Tho' we try to readjust them
        There they are among the stars.

Lives of great men all remind us
        We can write our names on high,
And departing leave behind us
        Thumbprints in the FBI.

FROM PING-PONG TO PEKING

Damn tricky these Chinese,
   But Dicky never knew it—
They built a better Mao-trap,
   He beat a pathway to it.

PALM SUNDAY 1972

Hail the season with artillery,
   Pour the hemlock—sip it, gulp it.
Berrigan is in the pillory,
   Messiah Moon is in the pulpit.

Christ must surely rise this one day
   To reflect on napalm Sunday.

DEFICIT

Nixon went to church each week
His conscience to release;
He sang his psalms
While dropping bombs,
And banked on God for peace.

He didn't think his prayers were odd,
But he awoke one dawn—
To find that his account with God
Was sadly overdrawn.

AND NOW, A MESSAGE FROM YOUR SPONSOR

Each time I hear some master voice
From out the oval room,
My trusting soul does not rejoice,
My heart is steeped in gloom.
And tho' the rhetoric scales the heights
Of righteous saintliness,
It's not the voice of the Bill of Rights
Or the Gettysburg Address.

When as for strength I turn the dial
To Rev. Billy Graham,
A biblical cascade of bile
Engulfs my fragile frame.
For tho' he is the very fount
Of love and Gilead balm,
I hear no Sermon on the Mount
Or the voice of the 23rd Psalm.

WATERGATE NURSERY RHYMES

I

Sing a song of politics
    With bottles full of rye,
Fourteen hundred delegates
    That anyone can buy.
When the voting opens,
    The price begins to rise—
And this, my little citizens,
    Is called free enterprise.

II

There was an old woman
Who lived in a shoe,
Her home was bombed out,
What else could she do?
Then her shoe was bombed out,
She had nowhere to stay,
So now she lives
In a green beret.

III

Simple Simon
Met a pieman
Going off to war,
Said simple Simon
To the pieman,
"What are you fighting for?"
"I fight for the great U.S.," he said,
"For the U.S. Commonweal;
For U.S. Rubber,
And U.S. Oil,
And especially U.S. Steel."

ABOUT FRED

What fun to have a playful mind
    To spend your leisure time in,
To hunt a word, and chase a thought,
    Or catch a little rhyme in.

To commandeer the alphabet
    With majesty and art,
And make the *word* become the *world*,
    And *earth* become the *heart*.

ADVERBS

WHERE and WHEN
    Are lost in space.
THERE and THEN
    Do not embrace.
So before we disappear
Come sweet NOW and kiss the HERE.

BEWARE OF THE DOGMA

The soma faces life with dread,
    The psyche fears each minute,
We suffer less from a cold in the head
    Than a new idea in it.

VIVA LA GRAPPA

Till Manischewitz aged it here
    Wine had been a foreign juice.
Now the poets all can cheer,
    They've found a rhyme for "orange juice."

INSCRIPTION ON A FLYLEAF OF THESAURUS
TO AN UPCOMING LYRICIST

Between the covers of this thesaurus
Is every lyric, verse, and chorus,
Of any song you think is fittin'
To be written.
All you do is just unite
The words that you would like to write.
They're all in here—precise—exact—
But you must know which to subtract.

POSTERITY IS RIGHT AROUND THE CORONER

Why should I write for posterity?
What, if I may be free
To ask a ridiculous question,
Has posterity done for me?

SAID OLIVER WENDELL HOLMES*

"Whenever God sculpts an artist
He gathers the chips that fall,
And out of them sculpts the critic . . ."
And that should explain it all.

*Note to critics: Blame him, not me.

TO THE CARTIACNIK

The golf course is so full of hills,
    The holes so far apart,
Before the heart resorts to pills,
    Be smart and hire a cart.

Don't push the pump that feeds the foot,
    But heed this little verse,
Before you putt, be sure to put
    The cart before the hearse.

SIXTEENTH-CENTURY DROPOUT

The bard of Avon never went to college,
    Never studied drama, grammar, art,
And yet could quote most every word of Shakespeare--
    Practically by heart.

**"GROW OLD ALONG WITH ME!
THE BEST IS YET TO BE."**
—Robert Browning

Come sit with me where dreams are spun
In the glow of the geriatric sun,
    And watch the lazy day go—
You with your aching ganglion
    I, with my lumbago.

TO WOULD-BE LITTERATEURS

If you crave to be an author,
    Or a superluminary,
In that incandescent circle
    Of the ultraliterary,
You've no need for erudition,
    Or a large vocabulary
If a blue-eyed gal named Sally
    Is your private secretary.

You can be a glowing poet
    Luring people to Brentano,
Or a lyric name engraved
    Upon the songbook on a piano;
You can be an instant playwright
    Witty, slick, contemporary—
If a slim-hipped gal named Sally
    Is your private secretary.

Who needs syntax?
Who needs spelling?
For the song
Within you dwelling.
When the muse
Becomes compelling
Put your faith in our good fairy.

You will find yourself dictating
Verses bright and scintillating,
Into eyes that know the merry
Secrets of a secretary.

WHEN THE MUSE IS AWAY FOR THE WEEKEND

Life is transient. Time is fleeting.
Dreams are drumbeats not worth beating.
Something in me keeps repeating
Is this quatrain worth completing?

WALLPAPER

DESIGNED FOR
THE PENTAGON

NATIONAL SECURITY

Mass the missiles,
Draft the boys,
     Pile the rockets high.
Build the bombers,
Load the bombs,
     Till they span the sky!

The Armageddon days have come,
     But one thing's very clear—
There's no defense that's strong enough
     To save a folk from fear.

Build pentagons and armories
     From Boston to La Jolla;
There is no fortress strong enough
     To placate paranoia.

FAIL SAFE

It's a hundred billion dollars
     Every year at your expense,
For the Pentagon to gadget up
     Our national defense.

But it's comforting to know that
     In the up and coming war,
We'll be dying far more safely
     Than we ever died before.

CLASSIFIED LEAK

Russia has a secret weapon
   Which our Secret Service finds
Can reduce us all to robots,
   Wash our brains, or blow our minds.

It can turn us into morons,
   It can churn us into neuts—
Freeze our gonads, freak our psyches,
   Turn our brothers into brutes.

Our "intelligence" is spending
   Many billions in pursuit
Of what may some day destroy
   Our way of life and love and loot.

Won't the CIA be ripped off
   When it once begins to see
Russia's very secret weapon
   Is America's TV?

GET READY! AIM! SUBLIMATE!

To overcome his malice
Toward a disobedient phallus,
He joined the army where all gripes are stored.
He's a general now defending
His "honneur" with an unbending
Every-ready, every-steady Freudian sword.

TRUTH

Truth is a foreigner
    Under every dome,
Truth is a refugee
    Looking for a home.
Without flag or passport,
    Hounded, plagued, and banned,
Truth must be smuggled in—
    It has no fatherland!

Truth is a subversive,
    A super counterspy
No CIA or OGPU
    Can shoot or bribe or buy.
Truth is the little candle
    That throws its laser beam
And cuts the cancered darkness
    Out of the living dream.

DEDICATION FOR THE NEW CHAPEL BUILT
IN THE PENTAGON IN 1971

When the hawks begin to gather
      In the holy halls of mayhem,
To receive the hallowed blather
      Of the Reverend Billy Graham,
In his heaven old Bill Shakespeare
      Sadly notes the latest trends . . .
"Can this be the divinity,
      I said, would shape our ends?"

A NEW BALL GAME?

The Chinese are a playful race,
Their apothegms far flung.
Their leaders all read poetry
      And all quote Mao Tse-tung.
Once Mao ad-libbed an epigram
That rang a global gong:
      "There's less to be won
      From the bang of a gun
Than there is from the ping of a pong."

A SONG A CHILD COULD SING

I blew a song into the air,
    A jingly little thing;
A simple song, a cheerful song
    Of love and star and spring.
A lilting and a laughing song—
    A song a child could sing.

It flew out of my window
    And scampered down the lane,
It caught the coattail of a breeze
    And rippled through the rain—
And everyone who heard it, stopped
    To whistle its refrain.

It reached a music broker
    On a noisy city street
Who photographed the soul of it
    Upon a music sheet;
And on a vinyl plastic disc
    Enshrined its rhyme and beat.

Then strings, and drums, and clarinets
    Unleashed it everywhere:
Through microphones, on microwaves
    Through supersonic air,
Down chimneys all antennae-decked
    In every thoroughfare.

And feet that never danced, essayed
　　　The light fantastic flip,
The lover who was shy before
　　　Found words to warm the lip.
On land, and sea, the melody
　　　Brought heart to shack and ship.

Then Gods of mighty slogans, high
　　　In glassed Olympian floors,
Linked the magic of the music
　　　To the merchants' metaphors,
And the hucksters and the hawkers
　　　Now became its troubadours.

Till consumers, in the spell of
　　　Its subliminal reprise,
Flocked to buy the anti-pain,
　　　The anti-sneeze, the anti-freeze,
The high collateral, low cholesterol
　　　And the neo-calories.

Togetherness and nicotine
　　　Entranced the buying throng.
Foreverness and loveliness
　　　Were packaged all day long;
And all were ushered in upon
　　　The wings of my small song.

The marts of commerce flourished!
　　The dividend divine
Rose up like Christ at Easter—
　　Soap up seven! Soup up nine!
While across the Wall Street heaven
　　Sunbeams formed a dollar sign.

And the patron saint of song, whose
　　Ways with copyrights are lax,
Smiled on me, and royalties
　　Rolled in, in bulging sacks.
With some for me . . . A *bit* for me,
　　But most for income tax.

The Treasury was happy
　　As a treasury could be,
For admirals and generals command
　　A handsome fee
To find strategic methods for
　　Annihilating me.

But to find strategic methods
　　Takes a heap of royalties;
So my taxes went for flying-flames,
　　And other sorceries
To test upon a village—
　　In some land beyond the seas.

Technology, and science, and a little
    Lyric rhyme
Conspired to blow some children
    Into space and out of time!
Now who's to sing a song again,
    In such a day and clime?

O muse, where is your sweet repose?
    O world, where is your spring?
To think that I could ever do
    So villainous a thing
As write a little laughing song—
    That any child could sing.

VICTORY MARCH

Whom are the bugles blowing for
    In the purple heart brigade?
For Johnny who is home on leave . . .
For Johnny with the empty sleeve . . .
    For Johnny on parade.

Whom are the banners flying for
    In the gold oak leaf brigade?
For Lenny who will never dance . . .
For Lenny with the legless pants . . .
    For Lenny on parade.

Whom are the church bells ringing for
    Above the flags that wave?
For boys who'll never march again
Through what triumphal arch again? . . .

Whose bishops blessed their bravery,
Whose Gods assured them victory,
Whose rulers gave them land, i.e., . . .
    In some dark distant grave.

ONE SWEET MORNING

Out of the fallen leaves the autumn
    world over,
Out of the shattered rose that will
    smile no more,
Out of the embers of blossoms and ashes
    of clover
Spring will bloom—one sweet morning.

Out of the fallen lads the summer
    world over,
Out of their flags plowed under
    a distant shore,
Out of the dreams in their bones buried
    under the clover
Peace will come—one sweet morning.

    "One sweet morning
      The rose will rise
        To wake the heart
          And make it wise!"

This is the cry of life the winter
    world over,
"Sing me no sad amen, but a bright encore!"
For out of the flags and the bones
    buried under the clover,
    Spring will bloom
      Peace will come
        One sweet morning—
          One sweet morning.

VALENTINE FOR EDELINE

St. Valentine, St. Valentine,
    For you a toast in vino!
To think that after fifty years
    I still am her bambino.
Though hair denude my forehead,
    And age betray my spine,
I'm still her Valentino,
    I'm still her Valium-tine.

TO HARRIET

Dear Harriet Van Horne
    We like you.
We like your style—your warmth—your scorn—
    Your IQ.

We prize your prose, we praise your pen
    To all your words we say "amen"
    And so again—and yet again
    We like you.

TO KAY HOLABIRD
(THE BELLE OF BENNINGTON)

Shall I compare thee to a Shakespeare sonnet?
Thou art more lusty-busty, more embraceable.
Some men are hooked on rhyme and swoon upon it—
I swoon on thee. Thy lips are less erasable.

Sometimes a phrase the icy spirit singes,
And oft doth metaphor the mind beguile;
But thy gold brow and Viking eye unhinges
The heart that knows thy touch, thy clutch, thy smile.

The trochee, dactyl, and iambic meter
Give wings to words that up to heaven go;
But benisons from Bennington fall sweeter
On denizens upon the earth below.

No mighty line—no holy writ nor word
Can soar above the hallowed Holabird.

INSCRIPTION ON AN ALBUM
TO JUDE

It would have been hard
On the poems of *the bard*,
And the songs of the bees and the birds too,
If the lyrics I write
Had the beauty and bite
Of the girl I am writing these words to.

TO LILY OF THE GALLERY

She stands in awe before each masterpiece
As Keats with urn, Copernicus with star,
And sighs at every Monet and Matisse,
And swoons at every Rembrandt and Renoir.
Her star-moist eyes absorb each subtle speck
That kissed the brush of Gauguin and Van Gogh.
Somewhere, up there, El Greco and Lautrec
Shine bright in halos that reflect her glow.
This worshiper should someday have the grace
To look into the mirror, and take thought,
And note the smiling soul that lights her face—
The soul that L. da Vinci never caught.

Then let her challenge Rembrandt and his troop
And dare them re-create her chicken soup.

THE GIRL THEY LOVE TO TOUCH

I'm her slim Santa Claus
For each crusade and cause
So her conscience can rest and sleep easy—

For I am the mister
Who married the sister
Of Francis the Saint of Assisi.

TO EDELEE
(IN MARTHA'S VINEYARD)

When she is alone
On our hill by the sea,
These are the things that worry me:

Is the screen on the hearth
When the fire is in it?
(*Is she worshiping me every day, every minute?*)

Has she fallen asleep
With the light in the socket?
(*Would the key I once held to her heart still unlock it?*)

Has she slipped on a rug?
Left her watch in the bath?
(*Does she wish it were I shouting "Puss"—on the path?*)

What visitors now
Is she having to nurse?
(*Does she still think that Shakespeare's as good as my verse?*)

Have the batt'ries that
Juice up her Buick corroded?
(*Does she look at my photo—and pronto get loaded?*)

Has the furnace been checked?
Has she turned off the oven?
(*Is she hep to this septuagenarian's lovin'?*)

Does she water my lilacs,
Clematis and berries?
(*Or search for my face—on all incoming ferries?*)

Oh plumbing, oh pressure,
Oh mystery noises!
(*Will she ever know truly whose heart this old boy's is?*)

When she is alone
On our hill by the sea,
These are the things that worry me!

TO EDELEE
(AT MOUNT SINAI HOSPITAL)

The muse has left my bed and board,
    The flame has fled my fire . . .
Lost, lost is every silver chord
    That graced my joyous lyre.

My melody is out of tune,
    My beat is out of time.
My word is out of reason
    And my reason out of rhyme.

Oh Moses, where Mount Sinai stands,
    Apply your holy art—
Bring back her sweet commandments
    That command this minstrel's heart.

Forgiving with your blessed staff
My worshiping the golden laugh.

NOTE ON DOOR
TO EDELEE
ON HER RETURN HOME

Let the boudoir lose its sadness!
   Let the kitchen shed its gloom!
Let the lilt of bubbling gladness
   Shake the walls of every room.

Let the ivy climb the ceiling
   As her shoe steps through the door,
Let the goldfish leaping, reeling,
   Glide across the vinyl floor.

Never more will shelf be fruitless,
   Bulb be dark or stove be cold.
Nevermore will life be bootless—
   Edelee has joined the fold!

Let the phone bells all be tinkly
   And the TV songs bel canto,
Bring her good news, Mr. Brinkley,
   Mr. Buckley—*scram*—but pronto!

TO MARY McGRORY
(UPON WINNING THE PULITZER PRIZE)

Sing hey ding-a-derry
   For Mary McGrory.
Mary contrary
   To tyrant and Tory.

Siren of sanity,
   Foe of buffoonery,
Shield of humanity
   From pentagoonery.

Eyes over which none can pull
   The old wool. It's her
Shavian wit—makes her fit
   For the Pulitzer.

Cheers for her peers
Who have honored and chosen her.

Praise for the pen
From which flows the brave prose in her.

Prize for the wise
Irish twinkle that glows in her.

Mary McGrory,
More glory
   To you.

TO MYOPIA*

Look you the goddess I hail with "hosanna,"
  Wisdom's Athena . . . beauty's Lucrece,
Forehead of Juno and limbs of Diana,
  Face . . . all the grace and the grandeur of Greece.

Out of what sky falls this heavenly body?
  Out of what star glows this heavenly flame?
Light for the mirthless, the earthbound, the shoddy,
  Beacon for poets who reach for her name.

Muse! Help me toast this celestial phenomenon.
  Maestro! A chord that will echo through time.
Roget! The book . . . for I feel a song comin' on.
  Shelley! Oh where is that deathless new rhyme?

Who in this hour of Dacron and Nylon
  Could conjure up seraphim frolicking free,
Or ever believe that an angel would smile on
  A clayfooted, clodhopping clinker like me?

Who would have guessed that his *Dolce Divina*,
  Every man's cynosure, every man's wish,
This hallowed madonna, this haloed bambina . . .
  Is Itkeleh Ruchel from Grand Rapids, Mich!

*The real Goddess of Love

THE EYES HAVE IT

To Aleine
I look into your glory eyes of grey—
And heaven is here on earth, and here to stay.

To Barbara
I look into your blessed eyes of brown—
I hear the angels sing all over town.

To Jeanne
I look into your dazzling eyes of green—
And now, I vow, it's paradise I've seen.

To Madeline
I look into your bonny eyes of blue—
I know there's no hereafter after you.

There is a moral to this verse and 'tis:
We're living on a slightly fickle star,
And paradise (whatever that is) is
Wherever you (whoever you are) are.

TO MARGE, AGE TWO

Who gave you beauty surely knew
That vastness that is heaven's blue.

Who crafted you did not forget
The softness of the violet.

Who dabbed with light of dawn your eye
Mixed chromosome with azure sky.

Whose artistry now through you beams
Once dipped her brush in other dreams.

Your mother (may her tribe increase)
Might have evoked a masterpiece.

If rompers didn't soil so soon
Or dried themselves beneath a moon!

Will you appreciate, my dear,
For you she spurned a great career?

TO JIMI

I do not think that I can write
A poem as sprightly as this sprite.

What poet, pray, can sonnetize
The sonnets mirrored in her eyes,

Or rhapsodize in dithyrambs
The swing of her iambic gams?

How rhyme, with rondel or rondeau,
The lyric under her chapeau?

What sweep of grace in triolet
Can match her serve across the net?

How sing with feeble chansonette
Her spirit, sparkle, soul, et cet?

I'd fling an epigram at her
In classical pentameter

But who can pen a poem to fit
A poem that is already writ?

TO JONO AT THIRTEEN

Bar Mitzvahs were made to remind you
Of a wealth of genetics behind you,
    That in you there flows a
    New Freud or Spinoza
To reshape the gods who designed you.

THE BALLAD OF MADELYN LEE

She dwells in the Village
  In Abingdon Square
The beautiful Madelyn Lee.
All telephone wires converge
  On her there,
The sweetheart of AT&T.

You ask who she is? She's the soul of the city,
The sweetie committed to every committee.
The wife of Jack Gilford, the funny, the witty . . .
  The bountiful Madelyn Lee.

She solves all your problems
  Allays all your fears
And sets all anxiety free.
Just call her collect and
  The next voice you hear
Will be that of our Madelyn Lee . . .

"Does your friend need a job? Or a script? Or vasectomy?
Does your wife need a maid, or a quick hysterectomy?
Call me back in an hour . . . but don't send a check to me"
  Fabulous Madelyn Lee.

Loathers of women's lib
  Freedom and sex
Don't dawdle when Madelyn smiles.
When she pickets the White House . . .
  They run for the ex-
It to cover and lock up their files.

If you're planning a strike, or parade, she'll gung-ho for you,
Bus you to Washington—raise all the dough for you,
And while she's in prison—produce a new show for you,
　　　Improbable Madelyn Lee.

　　　When Joe (sic) McCarthy
　　　　　Came down from the Heights
　　　To investigate Madelyn Lee,
　　　She appeared in her tights
　　　　　With the whole Bill of Rights
　　　Tattooed on her plump potpourri.

She's the blond Joan of Arc ever rallying masses
To strike against war and political asses.
Men who'd never clink glasses with Jackie Onassis
　　　Make passes at Madelyn Lee.
　　　There's no sadd'lin' Madelyn Lee.

　　　So here's to the girl
　　　　　Of this wild half a century,
　　　Fabulous, fearless, and free!
　　　This nation will not be
　　　　　A fed. penitentiary
　　　As long as there's Madelyn Lee.

So let's tear a herring and toast it in wine for her,
Let Barnum and Bailey design a gay shrine for her,
And the zodiac light up a new neon sign for her—
　　　Lovable laudable,
　　　Bright and applaudable,
　　　　　And audible,
　　　　　Madelyn Lee.

TO WHOM IT MAY CONCERN

Marriage needn't be so glum
    Or full of dangers . . .
Sometimes, with luck, we do become
    Better strangers.

And then by some mysterious blendship,
Love will ripen into friendship.

FOR HUBY AND BILL AND LEW*
(IN MEMORIAM)

I like to think of a somewhere star
    On the brink of our galaxy,
Where friends can meet at a jovial bar
    And the food and drinks are free.

The drinks are free and the talk is bright
    And the view is a firmament view.
The kind of view you would say "just right—
    For Huby and Bill and Lew";

A view that might attract perhaps
    A most compatible crew,
Like Lincoln and Franklin and Shaw and chaps
    Like Huby and Bill and Lew.

*Leo Huberman, Bill Gailmor, and Lew Frank

I like to fancy them chuckling away
      (In words more deftly purled),
"How long does that minstrel intend to stay
      On that smogged-out, mucked-up world?"

And the gist of the simple answer is:
"You started a lot of unfinished biz;

We've got to build up on the ground you dug,
Get rid of the dirt still under the rug.

But we can't do that till we're rid of the rats,
And that, my cosmic friends, O that's

A task for an old pied piper who
Must earn his permanent firmament view

Before he can join the courageous crew
Of Huby and Bill and Lew."

EPITAPH

I've whittled my wit,
And whipped my rhymes,
For a small obit
In the New York Times.